Table of Contents

Acknowledgements

My love and appreciation to my beautiful daughter, Lori Lynn Gillies, whose contributions of her time and talent have been instrumental to the completion of this book and to Rae Edlin, Mary Kay Kimball, and all my Sisters in my Bible Study Group for their love, support, and encouragement.

Rejoice in the Lord always. I will say it again: Rejoice! Let your gentleness be evident to all. The Lord is near. Do not be anxious about anything, but in everything, by prayer and petition and with thanksgiving, present your requests to God. And the peace of God which transcends all understanding, will guard your hearts and minds in Christ Jesus.

Finally, my brothers, whatever is true, whatever is noble, whatever is right, whatever is pure, whatever is lovely, whatever is admirable-if anything is excellent or praiseworthy-think about such things. Whatever you have learned or received or heard from me,, or seen in me-put into practice. And the God of peace will be with you.

Philippians 4:4-9

Dedication

I dedicate this endeavor to the memory of my beloved son, Michael, who when diagnosed with terminal cancer said, "It is what it is" and bravely, graciously, and with anticipation...accepted God's call to come home. Because of testimonies heard at his memorial, many were led to Christ, thereby answering Mike's question, "What does God want from me?"

Explanation of the ...dots

Dots...know as ellipsis between the first and second part of your greeting is a sort of poetic license to enhance the sentiment. If the design on the front of the card has space for the first part of the greeting, then finish with the second part on the inside. Otherwise, your greeting may all be on the inside, still using the dots for emphasis and dramatic effect.

Name	Verse #	Date Sent

"A friend loves at all times." Proverbs 17:17

Chapter 1

Friendship/Encouragement

1. I hope you know...but if you don't...know how much I appreciate your being in my life.

2. Like Jesus...you're always there when I need guidance, comfort, understanding, forgiveness and hope...What a friend we have in Jesus, what a friend I have in you!

3. Because you believed in me...I believed in me...thanks for your encouragement.

4. When I need a good friend...it's nice knowing you'll always be there.

5. It's been a long time since we said "Hi" ...but not a day goes by that I don't think of you.

6. It's been such a beautiful day...wish you could have been here to share it with me...and you were...in a way...always in my thoughts, in my heart, in my dreams.

7. When you feel alone...you don't have to...I'll always be there for you.

Just the Write Words

Name	Verse #	Date Sent

"Perfume and incense bring joy to the heart, and the pleasantness of one's friend springs from his earnest counsel."
Proverbs 27:9

8. Remember all those fun times together...and the sad times...how you were always there for me and I was there for you...the laughter we shared...the sadness we shared...what memories our friendship has etched in our hearts, treasures never to be forgotten.

9. You brighten my day with your sunshine, you warm my heart with your love, you soothe my anxieties with your understanding, you give me strength with your encouragement.

10. Sometimes I wonder what my life would have been like had I never known you, your love, your tenderness and caring, your thoughtfulness and your sharing, you're always there when I needed you, your smiles to share with me and your tears to shed with mine. A friend but so much more than that. A bond friendship that seemed deemed by God to be the union of two spirits that, joined, makes our lives more enriched, our sorrows more bearable, our joys more appreciated. And then, to think that, I could have perhaps, never known you. So today I want to let you know I am happy knowing you, happier knowing you are my forever friend!

Name	Verse #	Date Sent

"A man of many companions may come to ruin, but there is a friend who sticks closer than a brother." Proverbs 18:24

11. You're a joy to know...to know you're my friend...a greater joy.

12. So you're not perfect...I already knew that and...I love you.

13. Wishing you this kind of a day: a watercolor memory, echoing friendship, reflecting love.

14. There was no way I could have chosen you to be my (brother/sister) but if I could have...I would have. And there was no way that because you are my (brother/sister) that you would also be my friend...but you are!

15. God bless you for the joy your friendship has brought to me.

16. Wish we were saying "hello" instead of "goodbye" ...you'll be missed.

17. Just about the time I think I can't make it...you appear in my life and everything seems to be all right again.

18. Remembering our yesterdays...helps me get through my todays.

19. It's comforting knowing that with you...I can just be me.

20. When my words come out upside down and backwards...it's nice knowing you always understand.

Name	Verse #	Date Sent

"Dear friends, let us love one another, for love comes from God." 1 John 4:7

21. You being so nice is...so nice and appreciated.

22. When I'm lonely and need to talk...you listen. When I'm confused and need to listen...you're always there with just the right words.

23. When you just need to talk...I'll listen. When you just need to know that someone cares...I do. And when my words are not just quite right...I know you'll understand.

24. When you need to know that someone really cares...think of me.

25. You brighten my day with your sunshine smile. You warm my heart with your unconditional love. You soothe my anxieties with your understanding. You give me strength with your encouragement.

26. Stop and smell the roses, watch the spider spin its web...know God's world is beautiful and with Him, nothing is impossible.

27. Would it make things better if I told you...it's all going to be okay?

28. And this is how I spell friend... (person's name) ...thank you for being who you are to me...now and forever.

29. God's blessings on your Birthday...And God has blessed me with the beginning of another year of your love and friendship.

Name	Verse #	Date Sent

"Therefore encourage one another and build each other up, as in fact, you are doing." 1 Thessalonians 5:11

30. I love talking with you...me listening to you and learning...you listening to me and understanding.

31. I'm looking at all the things you overlook about me...thanks.

32. Thanks for being wise...during the times I wasn't.

33. Thanks for steering me in the right direction!

34. When you didn't have to...you did...Thank you for caring.

35. In your widely diversified corporation of friends...I'm glad I'm a shareholder!

36. When you need me, I'm here...and can be there anytime.

37. How blessed you are to have so many loving friends...How blessed am I to be one of them!

38. How lonely life would have been...to go through life without a friend like you.

39. When you're ready to talk about it...I'm ready to listen.

40. What a beautiful world this would be...if everyone was like the friend you've been to me.

Name	Verse #	Date Sent

"As iron sharpens iron, so one man sharpens another." Proverbs 27:17

41. Your care and thoughtfulness continue to cheer me...a joyous reminder of how blessed I am to have you in my life.

42. Because of you...I'm a better me!

43. The very thought of you...brings quiet smiles, warm feelings, and gentle memories.

44. The friend I've learned to be to others...reflections of the friend you've been to me.

45. You've been through so much...and still you smile!

46. Every time I smile...I seem to be thinking of you...and every time I think of you...I smile.

47. A little bit of sunshine...a little bit of rain...gives me a beautiful rainbow to send to you, my friend.

48. Our lives have changed...our paths have led us in different directions...but I know our friendship is forever.

49. Somethings never change...so happy in our forever friendship.

50. Just taking a break in my busy day to let you know...I think about you often and when I do...I always smile.

51. When I feel alone and think that no one cares...I think of you and everything somehow feels better.

Name	Verse #	Date Sent

"Do to others as you would have them do to you." Luke 6:31

52. I know that you care and you know that I care... guess that's what our friendship is all about.

53. Yes, our lives have changed and our paths have led us in different directions...but I know that our friendship will be forever.

54. Thank you for understanding and helping me through a rough time.

55. For all the things I said...and for all the things I didn't say...I'm sorry.

56. A gentle touch of your caring...has made such a difference in my life.

57. Sometimes an arm around the shoulder, the touch of a friendly hand...a feeling like no other when you know your friend understands.

58. I like you because...You like me even 'tho... guess that's what our friendship is all about.

59. When you need to know that someone really cares...think of me.

60. I've been busy through the day and I know you have been busy too, but there was a minute or two that I thought about you and somehow knew that you were thinking about me too... Isn't our friendship great?

61. Just to let you know I think about you often... and wish we weren't so far apart...

Name	Verse #	Date Sent

"My command is this: Love each other as I have loved you. Greater love has no one than this: to lay down one's life for one's friends." John 15:12-13

62. Thank God for you...I never could have made it without you!

63. Hi there, Mom/Dad...how's my best friend today?

64. Your friendship, your love, your caring...has made such a difference in my life...and I thank God every day for His bringing you into my life.

65. Your care and thoughtfulness continue to cheer me...A joyous reminder of how blessed I am to have a friend like you.

66. It's comforting knowing that with you...I can just be me.

67. Who you were yesterday...is not what you have to be tomorrow...I'll help you in any way that I can.

68. Months go by when I don't see you...but not a day goes by that I don't think of you. You are such a special person to me.

69. The times we've shared have made happiness happier...and sadness, easier to bear.

70. When you need me...I'm here...and can be there...anytime.

71. Life is a beautiful journey...but I would not have liked taking that journey without a friend like you.

Name	Verse #	Date Sent

"He who walks with the wise grows wise,
but a companion of fools suffers harm."
Proverbs 13:20

72. Was thinking about you today...it made me smile...remembering our fun times together.

73. If I had to ask for all the help you have been to me, I wouldn't have known how...Thank God, with you, I didn't have to.

74. When I needed to talk and be understood... you were there. When I needed to listen and learn...you were there. Know how much I appreciate your friendship.

75. You are such a beautiful reflection of Jesus in all that you do. I'm so inspired and blessed by your friendship.

76. You have filled my life with so much joy, so much love, so much understanding...I want you to know how much that means to me.

77. Those miles that have come between us... have only strengthened the bond of friendship between us...a friendship that is forever.

78. Today I thought about you...and all the smiles were reflections of all our happy times together...how I treasure those memories.

79. You made me smile again...thanks for caring.

80. I respect your decision...and if I can help...I want to.

Name	Verse #	Date Sent

"A righteous man is cautious in friendship, but the way of the wicked leads them astray." Proverbs 12:26

81. I don't pretend to know all the answers...but I'm a real good listener.

82. You don't have to face this all alone...Know that God will guide you and I'm beside you all the way.

83. We both know that having Jesus in our lives makes a difference...I know that having you in my life has also made a difference. Thank you for being my friend.

84. I know that with God all things are possible. I never could have made it without Him, nor without You.

85. It makes me feel good just thinking of you... Hope it makes you feel good to know that I am.

86. I have upon my finger a tiny piece of string, that helps me to remember things that need remembering. But sometimes I wish I had one tied in a magic knot to help me in forgetting things that need to be forgot. (Author Unknown)

    I want to say, "I'm sorry" ... Is there a way?

87. As you reflect on where you have been led these past months...may you face the challenges that lie ahead. I'm praying for your strength, understanding, and when appropriate, forgiveness and then joy.

Name	Verse #	Date Sent

"Love does not delight in evil but rejoices with the truth. It always protects, always trusts, always hopes, always perseveres." 1 Corinthians 13:6-7

Chapter 2

Love

1. I didn't think it possible that you would be more lovely and more loved than you were this time last year...But you are!

2. Through all our yesterdays...through all our tomorrows...I don't know how I could ever love you more than I do today.

3. Can't imagine a world without music...can't imagine my world without you...I love you.

4. When twilight steals the brilliance of the day...I'll remember times shared with you... cherish memories etched in my heart and happily recall...once I was loved (by you).

5. Your friendship, your love, your caring...has made such a difference in my life...and I thank God every day for bringing you into my life.

6. So...you're not perfect...I already knew that and...I LOVE YOU!

7. It doesn't make any difference...It's okay...I still love you.

8. Just love me...and I can cope with all the rest.

Name	Verse #	Date Sent

"Dear friends, let us love one another, for love comes from God. Everyone who loves has been born of God and knows God." 1 John 4:7

9. I know I can't have it all...so I'll settle for the part that includes you!

10. All my smiles and even all my tears...are because of how very much I love you.

11. I promise...I will always be here for you...if need be, I'll always be there for you whenever and wherever...know the kind of love I have for you will never end.

12. Being with you...is my reason for being.

13. What the world needs now is a new calendar... filled with only Saturdays and Sundays and on each square, make a note: Love him/her (name) today.

14. When you need someone, let me be the one.

15. Like the rose...you bring beauty to my world.

16. You're more important to me than...me.

17. Every time I think of you...I smile. Every time I smile, I seem to be thinking of you!

18. For all the hearts and lives you touched with love...I'm glad mine was one of them.

19. Sometimes I wonder what I'm going to do with you...and then...Sometimes I wonder what I would do without you.

Name	Verse #	Date Sent

"Do everything in love." 1 Corinthians 16:14

20. Let's always make it Christmas...keep the fire burning, decorate our lives with love... exchange gifts of caring, and show joy in being alive in each other's lives.

21. I appreciate all you do and say...and for all you don't do and don't say. I love you!

22. The Seasons change...but never my love for you.

23. You're special in my life...special in my heart.

24. With you in my life...it's a beautiful world.

25. I feel loved...and it's all because of you.

26. Where I am is where I want to be...in your heart and in your life.

27. There's so much in life that can be shared...I want to share it all with you.

28. The best part of today was...the time I spent with you.

29. Looking back...life has been a beautiful and blessed journey...made even more-so with you being such an important part of it.

Name	Verse #	Date Sent

"For you created my inmost being; you knit me together in my mother's womb. I praise you because I am fearfully and wonderfully made." Psalm 139:13-14

Chapter 3

Birthday

1. In your garden of life...you continue to grow. May God bless you with all that brings joy to your heart, peace to your soul, and wisdom to your mind.

2. Thinking of you today as we wish you happiness, good memories of the day, joy in the planning of your tomorrows and, through it all, peace in your heart.

3. Wishing you all things bright and beautiful for always.

4. What's so special about today? YOU and it's your birthday!

5. You're the only one I can send this to...Happy Birthday Mom/Dad.

6. [Son-in-Law} You're our son in the morning... you're our son in the evening...Happy Birthday to our Son-In-Love.

7. Only once a year to celebrate your Birthday? No! I celebrate you and our friendship every day, but with special love sent to you today... on your Birthday!

Name	Verse #	Date Sent

"...your eyes saw my unformed body. All the days ordained for me were written in your book before one of them came to be." Psalm 139:16

8. God put (birth date) aside as a day He would send to earth the most lovable creation He had ever designed...that's YOU my friend! Happiest of birthdays.

9. Once upon a time... (birth date) ...You were born to be the beautiful person that you are today. So glad you're in my life.

10. Because this (#) birthday is a milestone in your life...I want to be just one of many to wish you continued Happiness, Good Health, and Love!

11. Have a blessed birthday my Forever Friend... God has blessed me with the beginning of another year of our friendship.

12. Happy Birthday! As you continue on your journey through life, may the memories and blessings of the passing years bring you joy and comfort.

13. Happy Birthday to Someone Special...It's another measure added to your melody of living. May your song always be in the key of "C" with no sharps nor flats and may your added lyrics be the beautiful thoughts that are wished for you from friends who love you as I do.

Name	Verse #	Date Sent

*"For through me your days will be many,
and years will be added to your life."*
Proverbs 9:11

14. Happy Birthday! Be careful when opening this card...It is filled to capacity with so much LOVE, GOOD WISHES, and BLESSINGS...I was fearful that it would not have enough postage, but if it needed more...You're worth it!

15. Every day is a new beginning in which to learn something new, to count our blessings that keep us aware of all the joys there are in life, to reflect on the miracle of life, realizing that love is the most powerful force and that love is meant to be shared. Today, on your Birthday, know how very much you are loved.

Late Birthday

16. (Name)...we didn't forget...we're just kind of slow! Happy Birthday...hope it was!

17. Am I too late to blow out the candles...or am I too early? Okay so it's not your birthday today, but hope the day is a beautiful one for you my friend.

18. I figured you probably didn't want to remember anyway, so in thoughtfulness...I forgot it too!

Name	Verse #	Date Sent

"My flesh and my heart may fail, but God is the strength of my heart and my portion forever." Psalm 73:26

Chapter 4

Get Well

1. You are not walking the road to your recovery alone...Know how blessed are you to have so many friends who are walking beside you in prayer for your complete recovery and...how blessed I am to be one of them!

2. A little bit of sunshine...a little bit of rain... gives me beautiful rainbows...to send to you, my friend.

3. I'm wishing away...all your hurts!

4. I'll feel so much better...when you do!

5. I see your tears...I'm sending you sunshine so... you will have rainbows.

6. It's okay to cry...wish I could be there with you to wipe away all your tears.

7. Happy, smiling, joyful...that's me when I hear you're feeling better.

8. When you are facing reality and all of it's frightening realities...Know I am here for you.

9. It may not be all right tomorrow...but it will be better. Trust in God and know I am praying for you.

Name	Verse #	Date Sent

*"A cheerful heart is good medicine, but
a crushed spirit dries up the bones."*
Proverbs 17:22

10. It always amazes me how God takes care of things that need to be taken care of...and all we have to do is trust Him.

11. Remember in the days ahead...That I will be with you whenever you need me. And remember I am keeping you in my prayers.

12. I heard you have breast cancer...yes, cancer in your breast, but you have Jesus in your heart... He will see you through and I will be there for you also.

13. Okay, where do we go to "get you well?" Dictionary says, "a shaft sunk unto the ground to obtain water, oil, etc." Okay, I'm out to find a "well" and when I do, I pray, it will work for you! Praying for you!

14. May hope cast its special light upon the path you are now walking and at the end of that path, may you know peace and healing.

15. Just so you know, I'm feeling so much better... knowing you are too! Praying for your continued healing.

16. When I hear your voice and see your beautiful smile then I will know my prayers have been answered.

17. Now, more than ever, put your trust in God and He will see you through this. Remember, He has told us that He is always with us and will never leave us.

Name	Verse #	Date Sent

"He heals the brokenhearted and binds up their wounds." Psalm 147:3

18. Please know that today, and tomorrow, and forever...I'm just a phone call away.

19. Through all this, God will give you a rainbow of hope. He has said, "Be strong and take heart all you who hope in the Lord." (Reference: Psalm 31:24)

20. As you recover from your [illness, surgery, accident] ...Remember the comforting words of our Lord, "Peace I leave with you, my peace I give to you. Do not let your heart be troubled and do not be afraid." (Reference John 14:27)

Name	Verse #	Date Sent

"May the Lord keep watch between you and me when we are away from each other." Genesis 31:49

Chapter 5

Missing you

1. Today I thought about you...as I did yesterday... as I'll do tomorrow...I miss you.

2. I knew I was going to miss you...I just didn't know it would be this much!

3. I'm here...You're there...I need to be there...or you need to be here...Miss you this much!

4. The next time my phone rings...I hope it's you.

5. I'm trying not to miss you...so far, I haven't succeeded!

6. Wish we were saying hello instead of good-bye...I will miss you!

7. Missing...all you are to me.

8. With you, having to say goodbye is...feeling lonely before I am alone.

9. It was such a good feeling seeing you again... can't wait for that feeling to happen again!

10. I didn't know what lonely was...'til I was alone without you.

11. I miss our times together...and wish all that was...could be again.

Name	Verse #	Date Sent

"I long to see you so that I may impart to you some spiritual gift to make you strong – that is, that you and I may be mutually encouraged by each other's faith." Romans 1:11-12

12. Just to let you know I often think of you...and often wish we weren't so far apart.

13. Why am I here...and you are there? I wish we could be together.

14. The sad part about seeing you again was... having to say goodbye again.

15. I never minded being alone...until alone meant being with you!

16. As we say "goodbye" ...I'll be waiting for the time when we can say "hello".

17. The words you're longing to hear...Are the words I'm longing to tell you. I love you so much and I miss you even more!

18. It's lonely here without you...I miss you.

19. I smiled today...because I was thinking about you.

20. Missing...all you are to me.

Name	Verse #	Date Sent

"So with you: Now is your time of grief, but I will see you again and you will rejoice, and no one will take away your joy." John 16:22

Chapter 6

Sympathy

1. The sorrow we share is for just a little while... the shared memories of living love is forever.

2. Your loss is immeasurable...but so is the love he/she left behind.

3. When someone you love becomes, now, just a memory...that memory is a treasure.

4. Rest easy, my friend, in the loving arms of Jesus and find comfort and peace in the promises of God.

5. Someday we'll understand...for now know my thoughts and prayers are with you.

6. Those who live in the Lord have not seen each other for the last time. (Author Unknown)

7. You now may feel alone, but remember, the Holy Spirit is with you, protecting your heart, giving you hope, and promising you'll be together...again.

8. As you fervently search your heart for answers... Remember God is walking with you. Know the promised peace of God that it may bring comfort to your heart and to your spirit.

Name	Verse #	Date Sent

"He will wipe every tear from their eyes. There will be no more death or mourning or crying or pain, for the old order of things has passed away." Revelation 21:4

9. For all of those who do not know what you are going through...there are...many of us that do. God Bless You.

10. Know how much you will miss her/him...How you feel so alone, but with God by your side – you never have to be alone. She/He would be grateful that you have turned to God because she/he knows that is the answer.

11. As you face the days ahead, know that God will be right by your side, giving your spirit strength, courage, and filling your heart with His love. Hope it comforts you to know that I'm praying for you.

12. May the blessed hope of tomorrow and the glorious promise of Heaven comfort you in the days ahead.

13. May you find comfort in the love of your friends...May you find peace in the love of your God.

14. May you find a blessed comfort in knowing [name] is now in the very presence of God for all eternity. This is the promise of our Lord and Savior Jesus Christ.

15. It's okay to cry...Wish I could be there with you to wipe away your tears.

Name	Verse #	Date Sent

"Blessed are those who mourn, for they will be comforted." Matthew 5:4

16. He/She heard the call... "Come to me all you who are weary and burdened and I will give you peace." (Reference Matthew 11:28)

17. He/She is at peace now in the very presence of God. May His words be comforting to you.

18. I pray that hope will awake with you tomorrow... and God's peace follow you throughout the days ahead.

Name	Verse #	Date Sent

"This is the day the Lord has made; let us rejoice and be glad in it." Psalm 118:24

Chapter 7

Spiritual

1. The only constant in our life is Jesus...and that may be all the joy we need.

2. My favorite prayer: "Show me your ways, O Lord, teach me your paths; guide me in your truth and teach me, for you are God my Savior, and my hope is in you all day long." Reference Psalm 25:4-5 NIV

3. Upon the cross...He died for me. From the cross...He lives for me. With the cross...I'll live for Him. Because of the cross...Eternity.

4. God had a wonderful plan in mind...when He gave us one day at a time. Find your strength in His love.

5. Blessing: Thank you for the food before us. Thank you for the friends beside us. Thank you for the love between us. Thank you for your presence among us. Amen. (Author unknown)

6. To Mom and Dad: I love you because my heart tells me to. I honor you because God commands me to. Reference Deuteronomy 5:15

Name	Verse #	Date Sent

"Delight yourself in the Lord and he will give you the desires of your heart."
Psalm 37:4

7. One of God's most precious promises: Jesus offers light for darkness, peace for strife, joy for sorrow, hope for despair, and life for death. "Peace I leave with you; my peace I give you. I do not give to you as the world gives. Do not let your hearts be troubled and do not be afraid." Reference John 14:27

8. He will always be there for us...and I'll always be there for you. Reference Isaiah 58:9

9. And I will pray for you. Reference James 5:14-16

10. If you need a helping hand...just ask me. Reference Matthew 7:7-8

11. The best is yet to come. Reference 1 Corinthians 2:9

12. I know it's been rough...May you find comfort in God's word. "Though I walk in the midst of trouble, you preserve my life; you stretch out your hand against the anger of my foes, with your right hand you save me." Reference Psalm 138:7

Your thoughts may say:

13. "This is just impossible", but God says, "All things are possible." Reference Luke 18:27

14. "I don't think I have enough faith", but God says, "I've given everyone a measure of faith." Reference Romans 12:3

Name	Verse #	Date Sent

"Be joyful always; pray continually; give thanks in all circumstances, for this is God's will for you in Christ Jesus." 1 Thessalonians 5:16-18

15. "I'm tired and worn out", but God says, "I'll give you rest." Reference Matthew 11:28-30."

16. "I'm not smart enough", but God says, "I will give you wisdom." Reference I Corinthians 1:30

17. "Nobody really loves me", but God says, "I love you." Reference John 3:16 and John 13:34

18. "I can't go on", but God say, "My grace is sufficient." Reference II Corinthians 12:9 and Psalms 91:15.

19. "I don't know how to do this", but God says, "I will direct your steps." Reference Proverbs 3:5-6

20. "I am so worried", but God says, "Cast all your cares on Me." Reference 1 Peter 5:7

21. "I am so anxious", but God says, "Do not be anxious about anything, give your requests to me." Reference Philippians 4:6-7

22. "I am not able", but God says, "I am able." Reference II Corinthians 9:8

23. "I'm afraid", but God says, "Do not fear, for I am with you. I have not given you a spirit of fear." Reference Isaiah 41:10 and II Timothy 1:7

24. "I can't forgive myself", but God says, "I forgive you." Reference I John 1:9 and Romans 8:1

Name	Verse #	Date Sent

"Two are better than one, because they have a good return for their work: If one falls down his friend can help him up."
Ecclesiastes 4:9-10

25. "It's not worth it", but God says, "It will be worth it," Reference Romans 8:28

26. "I can't do it", but God says, "You can do all things." Reference Philippians 4:13

27. "How will I do this", but God says, "I will supply all your needs." Reference Philippians 4:19

28. "I feel all alone", but God says, "Never will I leave you; never will I forsake you." Reference Hebrews 13:5

Name	Verse #	Date Sent

*"Children, obey your parents in the Lord,
for this is right." Ephesians 6:1*

Chapter 8

Mother's Day/Father's Day

1. Especially for you, (name)! I love being your Mother and as I watch you, I marvel at your compassion, understanding, and devotion in being a Mother yourself. I pray your children (insert child's name(s) here) know the treasure they have in you.

2. You are a beautiful Mother and I love being your Mother. I have learned so much from you. Your gentleness, your patience, your dedication and devotion to your children have been an inspiration to not only me but to so many.

3. Just for you on MOTHER'S DAY

   Through the years, you are my reason for striving to become the Mother I have been able to be. You continue to be my inspiration to attain goals I never thought I could, to become more of a Christian than I ever thought I could be, to be a better person than I never would have been without you, and I shall be eternally grateful for the joy that I have had in being your Mother.

Name	Verse #	Date Sent

"Honor your father and your mother, so that you may live long in the land the Lord your God is giving you." Exodus 20:12

4. Thank you for always making me look so good as your Mother. You are such a beautiful person and I wish I could take credit for that but I know that it has been God that made you into the gracious woman you are today and I'm so grateful to have been part of your incredible life. I love being your Mom!

5. For all you are to me...For all you've been to me...For all I've been able to be because of You...Thanks Mom/Dad, I love you!

6. You have been such an inspiration to me in all you do... I can only hope and pray that I may reflect in my life all your love, your caring, your integrity, your tolerance, your sympathy and understanding. You are such a tribute to God's special creation...my Mother/Father.

7. I said this a lot when I was a little girl..."I love you Daddy." Some things never change! I love you Daddy...Happy Father's Day.

8. I'm sure I told you yesterday...how much I love you and I would guess that I'll probably tell you the same thing tomorrow...But today is very special for me...cause I can tell my special Mother/Dad just how much I love you on this day.

Name	Verse #	Date Sent

"Children, obey your parents in everything, for this pleases the Lord." Colossians 3:20

9. This card is unique...'cause I can only send it to one person...YOU! Happy Mother's/ Father's Day!

10. Especially for you from Grandma's Girl...I know why you love me so much...'cause I'm your little girl's girl...and I love you so much 'cause you're my Mommy's Mommy.

11. I know it wasn't easy Mom, but I love you for bringing me up the way you did.

12. You taught me how to give...with your giving. You taught me how to love...with your loving. You taught me to be kind...with your kindness. Thanks Mom/Dad...I love you!

13. I'm remembering all the special things you have done for me, the tender touches, the quiet understandings, the comforting love that has sustained me for so many years...I love you Mom.

14. On Mother's Day...You gave me life...Then taught me how to live it...You gave me love... Then taught me how to share it. Happy Mother's Day...I love you.

15. You were always there when I needed you... Know I will always be there when you need me. In gratefulness to you on this Mother's Day.

16. The Mother I've been able to be...Is a reflection of the Mother you've been to me.

Name	Verse #	Date Sent

"As a father has compassion on his children, so the Lord has compassion on those who fear him;" Psalm 103:13

17. Mother/Father...a priceless treasure of committed love between mother/father and child that reflects the ultimate bond of love in God.

18. For you dear daughter/son...You have made my being a mother/father all I dreamed it would be. You are so loved.

19. Now that you know what it really means to be a Mother/Father...You then must also know how very much you are loved.

20. For all the special things you do to help me make my dreams come true...Thanks Mom/Dad, I love you. Happy Mother's/Father's Day.

21. The Bible says: Honor your Father and your Mother...When you had to be both to me...Know how much I appreciate all you have done. (Reference: Exodus 20:12)

22. To my Grandma on Mother's Day...You're the best 'cause you gave me such a wonderful Mommy/Daddy. I love you.

23. To my Grandpa on Father's Day...You're the best 'cause you gave me such a wonderful Mommy/Daddy. I love you.

24. Hope this card makes you smile, Grandma/Grandpa...'cause it's filled with so much love for you!

Name	Verse #	Date Sent

"Listen, my son, to your father's instruction and do not forsake your mother's teaching." Proverbs 1:8

25. "You always said "Mother/Father knows best."
    And now...I know you did! Thanks for all your
    loving guidance.

26. For my Beloved Mother/Father on Mother's/
    Father's Day. I pray that someday I may be
    to my children...the Mother/Father you've
    been to me!

Name	Verse #	Date Sent

"For this reason a man will leave his father and mother and be united to his wife, and the two will become one flesh."
Ephesians 5:31

Chapter 9

Wedding/Anniversary

1. May the years that lie before you...forever reflect the beauty of this day.

2. Today...together...the beginning...of your beautiful tomorrows.

3. You've been the joy of our lives...He's/She's been the joy of theirs...May you both find special joy in each other's lives.

4. If I could choose again...I would still choose you! Happy Anniversary.

5. May this beautiful day be just the beginning of so many beautiful tomorrows together.

6. Through all our yesterdays...through all our tomorrows...I don't know how I could ever love you more than I do today.

7. Can't imagine the world without music...can't imagine my world without you...I love you!

8. When twilight steals the brilliance of the day...I'll remember times shared with you... cherish memories etched in my heart and happily recall...once I was loved by you.

Name	Verse #	Date Sent

"May he give you the desire of your heart and make all your plans succeed."
Psalm 20:4

Chapter 10

Graduation/Retirement

1. On your graduation...a time for reflections of all the good times that have been...A time for celebration for all the good times that lie ahead. Congratulations!

2. As you graduate...it's another measure added to your melody of living. May your song always be in the key of "C" ...without any sharps or flats and may your added lyrics be the beautiful thoughts that are wished for you from friends who love you as I do.

3. "Oh the satisfaction that is mighty sweet to take...when you reach a destination that you thought you couldn't make!" (Jody Menegatt 1952)

4. Now that you have graduated...Open your Book of Life, tear out all the old pages filled with meaningless thoughts, insignificant regrets, understood mistakes, inconsequential failures, and un-realistic dreams. Now that your book has become less heavy...it will be much easier to carry.

5. Consider this Day: It is the tomorrow that you didn't think would happen yesterday.

6. You should be very proud of you...I am! Congratulations

Name	Verse #	Date Sent

"For I know the plans I have for you, declares the Lord, plans to prosper you and not to harm you, plans to give you hope and a future." Jeremiah 29:11

7. I always knew you could do it...now you know it too!

8. The you, you were... The you, you are... The you, you are becoming...It's beautiful watching you grow.

9. Everyday a new beginning in which to learn something new, to count your blessings that keeps you aware of all the joys there are in life, to reflect on the miracle of life, realizing that love is the most powerful force and that love is meant to be shared. Today know how proud I am/we are of you and how much you are loved.

10. Today will be the yesterday you'll dream about tomorrow.

11. As you Graduate/Retire...Don't look back unless you can remember the joy and forget the sad. Don't look ahead unless you can see all the happiness that waits to be had.

12. Your tomorrows will always be reflections of your yesterdays...so be wise in your todays.

13. Remember your yesterdays...learn from them. Live your todays...enjoy the now. Dream your tomorrows...be the YOU, you want to be.

Name	Verse #	Date Sent

"The Lord will guide you always; he will satisfy your needs in a sun-scorched land and will strengthen your frame. You will be like a well-watered garden, like a spring whose waters never fail."
Isaiah 58:11

14. Congratulations on meeting the challenge and attaining your goal...May your future see all your dreams come true.

15. As the vision of your future becomes ever more clear...may you find yourself walking closer with the Lord who will continue to guide you to your own success.

16. Remember all the plans you have made and all the dreams you made come true...the future is yours to go as high and as far as you wish and I know success will be yours.

17. "And this is my prayer; that your love may abound more and more in the knowledge and depth of insight, so that you may be able to discern what is best and may be pure and blameless for the day of Christ, filled with the fruit of righteousness that comes from Jesus Christ–to the glory and praise of God." Philippians 1:9-11 NIV ...and this is also our/my prayer for you. We are/1 am so very proud of you in your accomplishments and wish you a lifetime of joyful fulfilment in everything you pursue.

Name	Verse #	Date Sent

"but those who hope in the Lord will renew their strength. They will soar on wings like eagles; they will run and not grow weary, they will walk and not be faint." Isaiah 40:31

18. A time for celebration for all the good times that lie ahead!

19. Remember in the days ahead... "'Tis better to have tried and failed than to fail because you didn't try." Best wishes for a wonderful future.

20. The seeds have been planted...Now grow...as we/1 know you will. Best wishes for a wonderful future.

21. Knowing how hard you have worked for this... You deserve all the happiness this accomplishment brings.

22. May the memories of happy times...make you strive for more. Congratulations.

23. You reached for a star...and captured it! Think how many stars there are in the sky...go for it! Congratulations on your Graduation.

24. As you begin a new journey – Remember the Word says, "Trust in the Lord with all your heart and lean not on your own understanding; In all your ways acknowledge Him, and He will make your paths straight." (Reference: Proverbs 3:6)

Name	Verse #	Date Sent

"I prayed for this child, and the Lord has granted me what I asked of him. So now I give him to the Lord. For his whole life he will be given over to the Lord." 1 Samuel 1:27-28

Chapter 11

New Baby/Baptism

1. It was love that put the child there...It was love that kept the child there...It was love that lives in the child...And with all that love this child shall be...tangible love in your arms.

2. As you hold little (baby's name) in your arms, you will be experiencing just the beginning of a love that just grows and grows...and as you share in that love, your lives/life will be so enriched that you will forever be praising God for bringing (name) into your lives/life.

3. Welcome (baby's name), God has chosen to bring you into a loving family. May your life be blessed as you grow in the love and knowledge of God.

4. Rejoicing with you in another one of God's miracles... "If you believe, you will receive whatever you ask for in prayer." Matthew 21-22 NIV

5. We share in your joy and in the blessing that God has, in His own time, given to you and your family.

Name	Verse #	Date Sent

"Peter replied, "Repent and be baptized, every one of you, in the name of Jesus Christ for the forgiveness of your sins. And you will receive the gift of the Holy Spirit." Acts 2:38

6. You waited patiently and God has rewarded you in His own time. When we trust in the Lord and know that there is a time for everything, we can experience the joy and peace that only God can give.

7. On your Baptism: Butterflies are free...and so are you...You have chosen to follow Jesus and His ways and ultimately know His many blessings, His promises, and His forgiveness of your sins.

8. As we celebrate your Baptism...always remember "Just as you have received Jesus Christ as your Lord and Savior, continue to live your *life* in Him, rooted and built up in Him, strengthened in the faith as you were taught and overflowing with thankfulness." (*Modified* Colossians 2:6-7 NIV)

9. Beginning your life anew with the Lord will fill your life with peace and joy.

10. God knew your child before he/she was born and He chose your family as the one who would best love and care for him/her as only you could, as you have, and as you will. I will keep you in my prayers; praying that God will sustain you with unsurpassed strength and peace in your hearts.

Name	Verse #	Date Sent

"My intercessor is my friend as my eyes pour out tears to God; on behalf of a man he pleads with God as a man pleads for his friend." Job 16:20-21

Chapter 12

Specialty Get Well

1. [Ear surgery] Ear-regardless, (name)...you're still ear-resistible ...do ya hear?

2. [Hip surgery] Hip Hip Hooray!! The hip pain has gone away!

3. [Foot surgery] Wishes for a toe-tal recovery... praying you'll soon be back on your feet and so hope you get a kick (ouch!) of this card...

4. Reminding you that "onions and bunions both rhyme and both bring tears all the time!"

5. [Knee surgery] Kneedless to say...if you kneed anything, we'll be glad to keep you knee-deep in chicken soup...or whatever you kneed to help you make a knee-jerk recovery.

6. [Cast] "Cast your cares on the Lord and He shall sustain you" Psalm 55:22

7. "Cast all your anxieties upon him. For He cares for you." I Peter 5:7 NIV

Name	Verse #	Date Sent

"In your anger do not sin. Do not let the sun go down while you are still angry."
Ephesians 4:26

Chapter 13

Tongue-in-Cheek

1. I know you thought I couldn't do it...And, of course, that just why I did!

2. You didn't think I could...but I did...and for just that reason!

3. Don't help me make a fool of myself...I can do that all by myself!

4. I hope your hurt doesn't hurt as much as mine.

5. It's not the things I've done I'm sorry for...It's the things I didn't do.

6. Just when I thought it was all right...it was all wrong.

7. Go ahead and burst my bubble! I will simply blow another!

8. Keep shutting me out...pretty soon I won't even bother to knock!

9. Go ahead and lock the door...Do you really think I'm never going to find the key?

10. I'll cry tomorrow...cause I've no tears left for today!

11. Remembering our yesterdays...help me get through my todays.

Name	Verse #	Date Sent

"Everyone should be quick to listen, slow
to speak and slow to become angry,"
James 1:19

12. The remembered yesterdays I was finally able to forget...all came back to me today!

13. Life without your love would have been easy... had I never known your love!

14. I told you I didn't like to make decisions... thanks for making it possible for me not to have to!

15. Go ahead and close the door...someday you'll want me to open it.

16. The you that was you...the me that was me... whatever became of our used to be?

17. If only I could take back all the things I shouldn't have said...and say all the things I should have said...would that make things better between us?

18. I'm going to get it all together, someday...hope you'll be there.

19. The older you are the more beautiful you have become...like I say today...you're downright GORGEOUS with a spirit that matches!

<u>Random thoughts by Sandy</u>:

"It's not so much that I didn't get any whipped cream...it's just that nobody noticed."

"It's not always easy being what you are not."

Chapter 14

Poetry by Sandy Juhola

"The words weren't always perfect. The words didn't always rhyme. But the words were only thoughts that spilled, and always, the thoughts were mine."

Our Prayer To You [1952]

Dear Lord,

Help us always to love as we do now. Guide us the right way in everything that we do. Let us always be together, even though miles may come between us. Let us forever trust each other under any circumstances. Let understanding and companionship strengthen our love. Keep us from any kind of temptation which might mar what we now have. Give us strength and courage to meet any problem, no matter how great. Let tolerance and intelligence guide our actions and decisions. Let our devotion to each other come before and above anything else. Never let us forget that it was you who brought us together; and when you feel that it is time for one of us to come to you, let us come to you together; for without each other, as without you, we are nothing. Amen.

<u>Sharing of the Sea</u> [1998]

I walk alone, along the delicate rim of the last wave, its foamy signature engraved upon the sand and feel the steady rhythm of the pounding waves as they blend with the same pounding rhythm of my heart and feel, that now, I am no longer alone.

She offers up her gift from the azure blue depths of the sea, gently delivered by one single foam-laced wave, lovingly left upon a soft pillow of shimmering sea-water, one perfect, unbroken, sunrise-pink colored shell.

I gather up this sculptured creation from its resting place, cupping it between my hands and holding it close to my heart. I feel the resounding murmurs of the sea echoing through my soul, embracing my very being, leaving me in peace.

<u>October Hill</u> [1951]

Everyone is sleeping, it is still
As I sit here on the side of a hill
With only the stars and moon to see
With only the wind to whisper to me.
Everyone has gone only night remains
Residing over this hill and plain.
How beautiful it is to sit and listen
To the growing grass and dew that glistens.
Everyone is quiet, I am alone
Just waiting for someone else to roam
and sit down beside me to watch the night

as it fades into darkness and then into light.
He would not have to walk with me,
nor would he have to talk with me,
but just sit here and think of life,
forgetting the days troubles and the strife.
To think of God, to wonder how He
ever thought to put on this earth you and me.
To look into the dark and see those things
the light of day never brings.
To listen to sounds coming forth from the dark,
to forget about time in its endless arc,
to breathe in fragrance of moonglow and stardust, to
be happy and carefree as the wanderlust.
Yet I wait all alone, here in the night,
and no one has yet come into sight
except for a bird flying overhead
and a falling star, a light now dead.
So I go on thinking and listening to sounds
all by myself with no one around
and I think to myself, how much you are missing: The
contentment of sitting and just reminiscing.
Everyone is sleeping, it is still
as I sit here on the side of a hill,
with only the moon and stars to see,
with only the wind to whisper to me.

Love's Masquerade [1953]

This isn't the way it happens in books, or the way the
poets describe it; it's all so different, I can't imagine
my falling in love so quiet.

When I first began to think of love and all its magic wonders, I thought that it would happen quick like a sudden bolt of thunder.

And my love, he would be so tall, so dark and so romantic; his kiss would be of passion and want and his arms strong and magnetic.

And whenever I would be with him stars would fill the sky, music divine and perfume sweet; this was my love and I.

How disillusioned a girl I was to think love could happen as this, for now the true meaning of love has found itself in us.

There is no madness about it. There is no wonder or awe; there is just the sweetness of your voice and the truth I never saw.

There is just the tenderness in your kiss; a gentleness in your arms; a feeling of joy in every glance and a smile so knowing and warm.

Yes, this is how it happened, not the way others try to portray it, for the love they know wears a masquerade and you have at last unveiled it.

You have shown me a real love that others have failed to see; Forever, unchanging, together as I love you and you love me.

A Bureau Full of Memories

Assorted buttons...in a box...un-used spools of thread...
faded and crinkled paper patterns...yards of mate-
rial, lovingly folded, reminders of little girl dresses...
the prom dress...the wedding dress...a bureau full of
fulfilled dreams and unfulfilled dreams...snaps and
hooks, lace and zippers...pins and needles...bits and
pieces of dreams...stashed away for a someday...or
maybe...just a garage sale.

Evening

It's evening, and the last faint light of a once flaming
sunset is fading. A lonely and darkening silence befalls
these rolling hills and all wait for morning to come.

The Owl Andirons at Our Cannon Beach House [1990]

They never cease their stately countenance... These
owls that guard so well that one more fire built within
their stone castle...Which one will this be for?

Warmth to ease the chill from a late-night walk along
the beach or waning coals just perfect for a marsh-
mallow roast...

Perhaps a practical fire so the furnace doesn't have to
work so hard...

Maybe a romantic atmosphere for a night of
lovemaking...

Maybe just something to gaze upon when the eyes grow weary of watching the repeating waves.

How many memories are etched along these walls? And still they stand. Silently watching the comings and goings of all who share this special hide-away... over a quarter of a century of watching love and life and growing.

Never smiling...but never frowning and always there.

An Afternoon at Cannon Beach

Listen to the stereo sounds of the waves crashing defiantly against the rocks and the shore...
Then watch them silently retreat to the sea.

Watch the children fly their kites...soaring like harnessed seagulls up to the clouds.

Splendor in the sheer physical warmth of the sun... penetrating deeper than you thought allowed.

Feel...and let sift through your fingers the glistening and sparkling sands that outshine any diamonds many ever cut.

Breathe in clean and cool salt-scented air.

Watch....and perhaps envy couples walking hand in hand along the water's edge.

See the charred driftwood...black carved monuments of an evening's bonfire on the beach...what memories are etched in that charcoal arch?

See Haystack Rock...not the way a thousand artists have interpreted it...but just as it is...as God put it there.

Share...if just for today,

sun...sights...sounds...seagulls...surf...sand...solitude...sensations.

Today will not happen tomorrow.

Today...this day...was meant for you...was meant for me.

Say "Hi" ...and this day will be made for us.

The Answer [1953]

Because men failed to understand; because they failed to try. You have been called away from me to fight beneath foreign skies.

They took you young and full of strength, they knew you were the best, they knew your body and your mind could meet the brutal test.

Then they placed in your hand a mighty gun, saying, "Here, soldier, go and kill" and you obey, for there it is law and will remain so until...

Men decide to stop awhile and listen, to try to under-stand; so that never again will you be taken from me to that distant land.

For someday soon you will return and all will be in peace. The gunfire, bombs, and all men's screaming will have, at last, been ceased.

And then if some should chance to ask you about how it ended and why, I know just how you'll answer for the same thoughts have I.

You'll say, "The answer is as old as time, but to know it many men have died. "Tis because men learned to understand, because my friend, they tried."

Autumn

It's the restless season. The changing leaves, no longer content with their constant green tinge, change their costumes to don gay and vivid colors; warm hues of red and gold. They leave the home they knew so well to find a new world, alas, only to find they are now dead and can never return again, but float on down that stream into which they fell and finally corrode and rot and lose their distinction, individuality and recognition into the earth from whence they first began.

My Night

In the aloneness of the night, the quiet time enfolds me. I feel the tranquil softness that settles and remolds me.

I'm different now and so serene. I see the precious treasures, treasures that by daylight hidden oft forgot and never measured.

I became aware and conscious of my whole self as one, awareness that never reveals itself in the lightness of the sun.

I love the dark, the silence that complete sweet solitude. I'm myself...and I like that, my own...my interlude.

The Difference

[Crooked River Ranch 1999]

I close my eyes and hear the sound of the surf and feel the breeze against my cheek, but the breeze is far too warm for it to be off the ocean and there is no salt taste...

And then I realize the sound is the wind sifting through the juniper bushes and any waves I might see are the waving "bunch grasses" swaying to the nudges of the warm winds.

Here, it is a constant, there is nothing new, it is the same as it has always been, as it will always be, the same unmoved rocks, the same sculptured trees, the same tufts of grass.

There...the scene is ever-changing, ever-new. No tide is the same, no shoreline exactly duplicated, sand dunes that change their shape with each new storm, new tides, new wild winds.

No rock stays in the same place (except for Haystack and Tillamook Head), and sea anemones and starfish trade dwelling places like vagabond travelers.

The sands drift from here to there, obeying the fickle winds, and there is always the taste of salt.

When It's Over

When it's over, there will be few who will be impressed that the stereo was dust free. There will be hardly anyone who knew, or much less cared that the dish-towels were neatly folded and in their proper place. And in this world of millions of people, who really cares that the kitchen floor shines from recent application of the top selling floor wax?

Yet, there is a person who will remember I took the time to listen...to really understand and feel. There are those, who when they really needed only me... I was there.

There were times when duties fell way to emotions and children's questions deemed more important than clean underwear.

Our Cannon Beach Tree [1982]

Still standing...

A defiant monument to memorable years, waiting and challenging that one last wind that will inevitably make it just one more piece of driftwood on the beach.

Still standing...

Hanging on, still inviting seagulls to perch for just a little while. Wish it could know that a caring someone preserved that sentry stance on canvas, complete with sunset colors it has seen for so many years.

Goodbye tree...you're missed.

Goodbye tree...you're remembered.

The Widow [2008]

One of them but way too soon
who chooses not to rise 'til noon,
who sits alone and twirls her ring
'round her finger, remembering
the days that traveled far too swift;
the memories that float adrift
through times and laughs and tears that fell,
remembering, now as evening swells
the heart with love that is forever
a heart that will the same...be never.

The Soldiers

Written by my brother, Jim Richards

I hear somewhere in a little town, on a sidewalk by a street,
a group of little boys playing soldier there and the marching of their feet.
They dream of being on a battlefield real and fighting for their home
or stationed in a far-off land, in Germany or in Rome.

I hear somewhere in a foreign land the marching of grownups feet
and the minds of men as they remember when they played soldier in the street.
But now they are in another land and the fight, it is real. They're fighting for those kids back home who haunt their memories still.

I hear somewhere in a distant land the marching of grown-up feet,
they died like men for the battle's end, now they're guarding Heaven's streets.
But often they gaze with a tearful eye to the world below their feet,
and bless the little children there who play soldier on the street.

My Brothers Graduation

The years go by so quickly
And faster still they'll fly
Now that you've reached that first plateau
Away up in the sky.

So many joys you've yet to learn
So many sorrows too,
But no matter what the future holds
I know you'll see it through.

And I know, too, that someday
I'll be prouder than all the others,
When I look up to life's highest peak
And see, standing there, my brothers.

Memories of My Father [1987]

Written by my brother, Jack Richards

I hear that distant song-voice now,
the chords still fill the air,
and leave my spirits soaring,
as if he still were there
among the chords, singing,
blending harmony with pitch,
the songs which swelled his heart and soul,
and made us all so rich.

Such lilting notes
have blessed us with
a loving memory,
God rest this gentleman of song,
God bless we say to thee...
you touched the chords of all you loved,
your spirit-song is free,
you left so much, but most of all,
you left your song with me.

<u>"A Sandyism"</u> [1969]

I remember when I was 22,
that was the year my waistline was too.
And now that I am 36,
that's what it measures 'round my hips.
But it's sad to face the fact, I must,
that my age will always be more than my bust!

About the Author

I have lived in Portland, Oregon all of my life, attending Beaumont Grade School, Grant High School and Oregon State University. Married, but now widowed, with two children. My love of writing has taken me down many avenues including poetry, children's stories, to writing and directing children's plays at Mountainview Christian Church in Gresham, Oregon.

I enjoyed my commission of writing verses for Jonathan and David's line of "Precious Moments" greeting cards and some of the sentiments are from my line of greeting cards, "Sincerely by Sandy" self-published in 1982.

This collection of sentiments spans over 70 years of creating special greeting cards for friends and family. Inspired by my friends to create this book, I journeyed on a virtual treasure hunt to uncover bits and pieces of words written on the backs of envelopes, crumpled cocktail napkins, lined notebook paper, sticky notes, even morsels transferred from the palm of my hand, anything available for my pen to record and capture a fleeting thought that might escape me and be lost forever.

I hope you will find inspiration in these words.

CPSIA information can be obtained
at www.ICGtesting.com
Printed in the USA
LVHW050840041220
673100LV00008B/156

9 781632 215499